Vampire Bats

ABDO
Publishing Company
A Buddy Book
by
Julie Murray

VISIT US AT
www.abdopub.com

Published by Buddy Books, an imprint of ABDO Publishing Company, 4940 Viking Drive, Suite 622, Edina, Minnesota 55435. Copyright © 2005 by Abdo Consulting Group, Inc. International copyrights reserved in all countries. No part of this book may be reproduced in any form without written permission from the publisher.

Printed in the United States.

Edited by: Christy DeVillier
Contributing Editors: Matt Ray, Michael P. Goecke
Graphic Design: Maria Hosley
Image Research: Deborah Coldiron
Photographs: Corbis, Digital Stock, DigitalVision, Mark Kostich, Photodisc

Library of Congress Cataloging-in-Publication Data

Murray, Julie, 1969-
   Vampire bats/Julie Murray.
      p. cm. — (Animal kingdom. Set II)
   Includes bibliographical references and index.
   Contents: Bats — Groups of bats — Vampire bats — What they eat — Bat wings — Roosting — Echolocation — Babies — How bats are helpful.
   ISBN 1-59197-313-9
      1. Vampire bats—Juvenile literature. [1. Vampire bats. 2. Bats.] I. Title.

QL737.C52M87 M87 2003
599.4'5—dc21

2003042585

Contents

Bats

    Bats have been around almost 50 million years. They are the only **mammals** that can fly. There are more than 900 kinds of bats. They live in many places around the world.

Bats are the only flying mammals.

Kinds Of Bats

The two main groups of bats are megabats and microbats. Megabats live in warm places in Asia, Africa, and Australia. They have big eyes and keen eyesight. Many megabats only eat fruit. So, many people call them fruit bats.

Most microbats are smaller than megabats. They have small eyes and big ears. Their wings are good for flying fast. Most microbats eat insects.

Most megabats (left) are bigger than microbats (right).

Vampire bats are microbats. They live in Mexico, Central America, and South America. Unlike other microbats, vampire bats eat blood. They are named after the imaginary vampire monsters.

Vampire monsters are not real.

What They Look Like

Vampire bats are furry. They may be grayish brown or reddish brown. They have pointed ears and a small, wrinkled nose.

Vampire bats

Vampire bats are small animals.

Vampire bats are small. They grow to become between two and four inches (5 and 10 cm) long. Adults weigh between one and two ounces (28 and 57 g).

Bats are the only **mammals** that have wings. A vampire bat's outspread wings are about 12 inches (30 cm) across. The wings have two layers of skin. This skin stretches tightly over a bat's outspread wings.

Resting bats fold in their wings.

There are four fingers inside each wing of the vampire bat. Bats also have a fifth finger, or thumb. A claw is on each thumb.

Bats have claws on their thumbs and back feet.

Eating

Vampire bats take blood from cows, pigs, horses, and other animals. They bite their prey with sharp teeth. Then, they lick up the blood. A vampire bat may return to the same prey night after night. Most animals do not feel the vampire bat's bite.

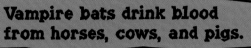

Vampire bats drink blood from horses, cows, and pigs.

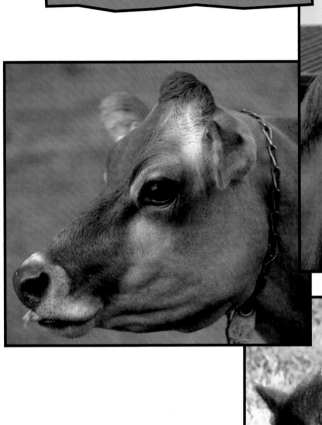

A vampire bat's bite is not deadly. But, some vampire bats carry **rabies**. Rabies is a deadly disease. A vampire bat can give rabies to the animals it bites. Rabies is a deadly disease for people, too.

Vampire bats can spread rabies.

Roosting

Bats sleep, or **roost**, during the day. They may roost in trees, barns, caves, or attics. A roosting place may have a few bats or thousands.

Vampire bats roost upside down. They hang from their back feet. A roosting bat often covers itself with its wings.

A roosting vampire bat.

Blind As A Bat?

Bats are not blind. They can see. Bats also use sounds to find their way. They will make sounds, then listen to the echoes. The echoes tell them the size and shape of what is ahead. This is called echolocation.

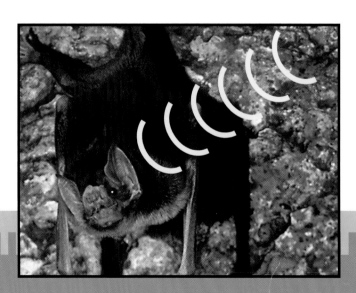

Bat Pups

Baby bats are called **pups**. A female vampire bat commonly has one pup at a time. Newborn pups are helpless. They need their mother's care.

Bat pups have strong feet and legs. They can hang onto their mother. Pups drink their mother's milk. They can fly after about five weeks. Vampire bats can live as long as 20 years.

How Bats Are Helpful

Bats help people in many ways.

Bats can be helpful in different ways. A special medicine comes from vampire bats. This medicine helps people with heart disease.

People look for bats in caves.

Many kinds of bats eat grasshoppers, beetles, and moths. These insects eat farm crops. Bats help farmers by eating these harmful pests. Some people keep bats nearby to kill mosquitoes, too.

Bats eat many pests, such as mosquitoes.

Important Words

echolocation using sounds and echoes to learn the shape and size of objects ahead.

mammal most living things that belong to this special group have hair, give birth to live babies, and make milk to feed their babies.

prey an animal that is food for another animal.

pup a baby bat.

rabies a deadly disease.

roost to rest or sleep. Bats roost during the day.

Web Sites

To learn more about vampire bats, visit ABDO Publishing Company on the World Wide Web. Web sites about vampire bats are featured on our Book Links page. These links are routinely monitored and updated to provide the most current information available.

www.abdopub.com

Index